POLAR

Published in 2015 by Cavendish Square Publishing, LLC
243 5th Avenue, Suite 136, New York, NY 10016

First Edition

CPSIA Compliance Information: Batch # WS14CSQ

Library of Congress Cataloging-in-Publication Data

Stefoff, Rebecca, 1951- author.
Polar bears / Rebecca Stefoff.
pages cm. — (Giant animals)
Includes bibliographical references and index.
ISBN 978-1-62712-963-3 (hardcover) ISBN 978-1-62712-965-7 (ebook)
1. Polar bear—Juvenile literature. I. Title.

QL737.C27S694 2015
599.786—dc23

2013050648

Editorial Director: Dean Miller
Editor: Andrew Coddington
Copy Editor: Wendy A. Reynolds
Art Director: Jeffrey Talbot
Designer: Joseph Macri
Photo Researcher: J8 Media
Production Manager: Jennifer Ryder-Talbot
Production Editor: David McNamara

The photographs in this book are used by permission and through the courtesy of: Cover photo by © Ardea/Watson, M./Animals Animals -- All rights reserved; age fotostock/SuperStock, 4; Ghedoghedo/File:Amphicyon ingens/Wikimedia Commons, 6; Fred Bruemmer/Photolibrary/Getty Images, 8; Daniel Eskridge/Stocktrek Images/Getty Images, 9; James Hager/Robert Harding World Imagery/Getty Images, 11; Nagel Photography/Shutterstock.com, 12; John Hyde/Alaska Stock - Design Pics/SuperStock, 13; Jack Dykinga/Photo Researchers/Getty Images, 15; Wayne R Bilenduke/Photographer's Choice/Getty Images, 16; taviphoto/Shutterstock.com, 19; JONATHAN DRAKE/EPA/Newscom, 20; Andy Rouse/The Image Bank/Getty Images, 21; Daisy Gilardini/The Image Bank/Getty Images, 23; Biosphoto/SuperStock, 24; Alaska Stock/Alaska Stock - Design Pics/SuperStock, 27; Wayne Lynch/All Canada Photos/Getty Images, 28; Gordon Wiltsie/National Geographic/Getty Images, 29; Thomas Kokta/Photographer's Choice/Getty Images, 32; Nick Garbutt/Science Faction/Getty Images, 34; USGS/File:Polar Bear Habitat.png/Wikimedia Commons, 37; Daisy Gilardini/The Image Bank/Getty Images, 40; Karen Kasmauski/Science Faction/Getty Images, 41.

Printed in the United States of America

CONTENTS

CHAPTER ONE

THE NEWEST BEAR

The largest bear in the world is the polar bear. This white giant of the north is also the newest bear. Today there are eight **species**, or kinds, of bears in the world. The polar bear was the last of these to appear.

How and when polar bears came into being is a puzzle that scientists are working to solve, but they do know that polar bears are the latest branch on a family tree that is about twenty-five million years old.

Clues to the history of bears come from two sources. One source is the **fossil** record. Teeth, skulls, and bones of extinct bear species have been preserved as fossils in many parts of the world—turned to stone over long periods of time as minerals seeped into them from the soil and water. The other source is deoxyribonucleic acid, or **DNA**, a **genetic** material within the cells of all living things that carries traits and features from parents to their offspring. By digging up and studying fossils of ancient bears, and by studying the similarities and differences in the DNA of living bear species, scientists are piecing together a picture of bear evolution.

The Dawn Bear

The ancestors of bears were a group of ancient **mammal** species that were **carnivores**, or meat-eaters. Around forty million years ago, some early carnivores developed into the first **canids**, or members of the dog family. Around twenty-five million years ago, a new branch appeared on the canid family tree. It was the **hemicyonids**, a scientific term that means "half-dogs." These ancient animals are also known as "dog-bears" because they had both doglike and bearlike features. Their teeth were similar to canid teeth, but they had the short, thick legs and heavy backbones that would become features of true bears.

One hemicyonid was a raccoon-sized animal called *Cephalogale* that spread through Asia and Europe. Over time, its eating habits changed. Scientists can tell from changes in its fossil teeth that it went from being a carnivore, eating only meat, to being an **omnivore**, or "everything-eater"—in other words, an animal that eats both meat and plants.

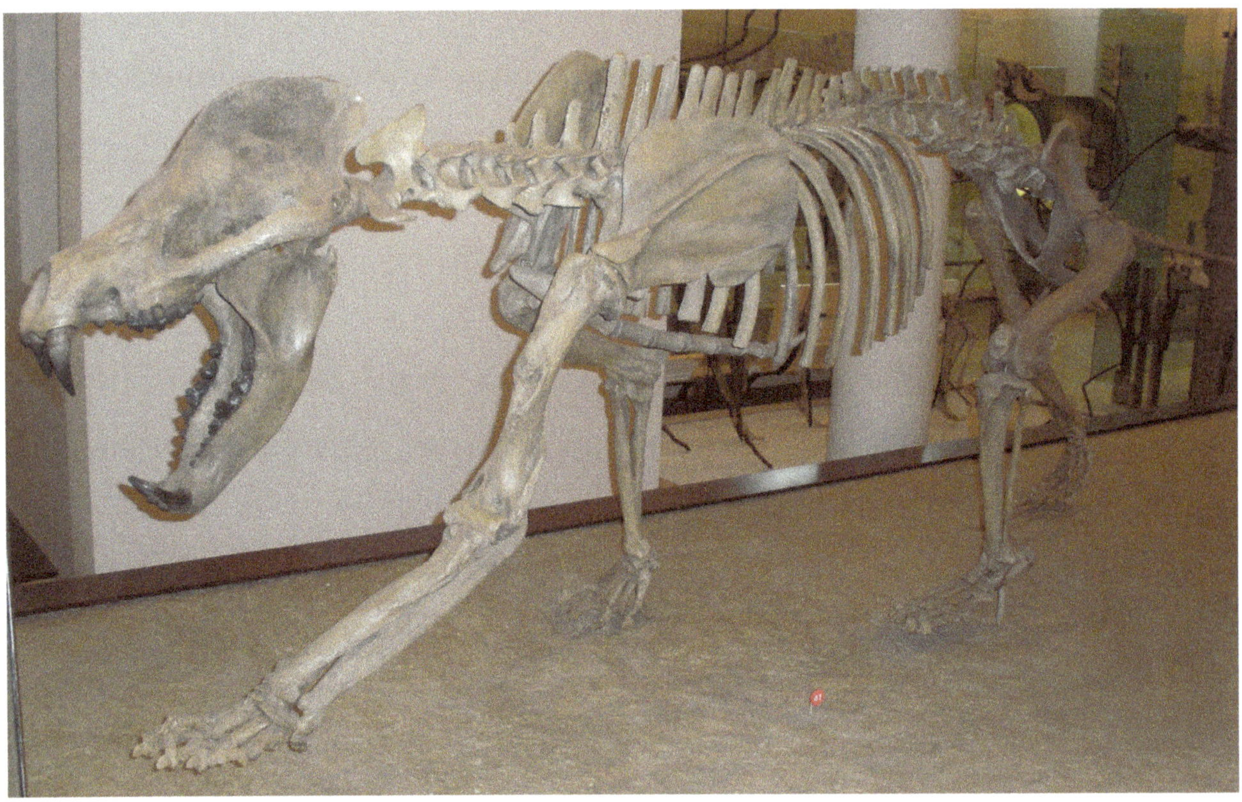

Some long-extinct species of carnivores blended the features of dogs and bears, which descended from the same distant ancestors.

By twenty million years ago, some descendants of *Cephalogale* had **evolved** into a new kind of animal. Scientists have grouped several species of this animal into a **genus**, or cluster of closely related species, called *Ursavus*. One species was *Ursavus elemensis*, a small, ground-dwelling omnivore about the size of a cat or small dog.

Ursavus elemensis was the oldest known true bear and a direct ancestor of all modern bears. It is sometimes called the dawn bear. Its descendants—many extinct species of bears and the eight species alive today—all belong to a family that scientists call the *Ursidae*. It is for this reason that a bear is also known as an **ursid**. Things related to bears can be called **ursine**. For example, this chapter is about ursine evolution, or the origin of bears.

Prehistoric Bears

The dawn bear gave rise to several subfamilies of bear species. The first subfamily to branch off, between nineteen and fifteen million years ago, was the giant pandas.

Five species of giant pandas are known to science, but four of them became extinct long ago. The lone survivor is the black-and-white giant panda of central China. Most scientists agree that pandas are bears, but they belong to a genus of their own. Because giant pandas have been evolving separately for many millions of years, they are different from all of the other living bears, which branched off the family tree a little later. Giant pandas, for one thing, are the only bears that are almost completely vegetarian. Their primary food is bamboo.

Between twelve and fifteen million years ago, the main ursid line split into two subfamilies. One subfamily lived in the Americas. The

Rock art in Alta, Norway, created as many as 6,000 years ago, shows prehistoric humans hunting bears.

other subfamily lived in Asia and Europe, although some species in this group later migrated to North America and Africa.

The ancient American subfamily of ursids is known as the short-faced bears. This group included the North American and South American giant short-faced bears, the Florida spectacled bear, and the South American spectacled bear. Only one species of this subfamily remains today: the South American spectacled bear. Its name comes from rings of pale tan fur on its face, sometimes around its eyes. Against the bear's dark brown fur, the rings make it seem as though the bear is wearing spectacles, or eyeglasses.

Between four and five million years ago, a bear species called *Ursus minimus* evolved in Europe. Weighing in at about 110 pounds (50 kg), this forest-dwelling bear probably looked like a smaller version of the modern American black bear. Three-fourths of the bear species that exist today—including polar bears—evolved from the descendants of *Ursus minimus*.

One of those descendants was the European cave bear. Much larger than *Ursus minimus*, it was about the size of a North American grizzly

The Biggest Bears of Past and Present

Polar bears are big. An adult male can weigh more than 1,760 pounds (800 kilograms) and measure more than 8 feet (2.5 meters) from its nose to the last bone of its tail. One male bear shot in the Arctic during the nineteenth century is said to have been even larger, weighing in at 2,200 pounds (1,000 kg).

Bigger bears once roamed North and South America. Scientists once believed that the largest bear of all time was the extinct North American giant short-faced bear. Experts think that the largest individuals in this species weighed about 2,500 pounds (1,130 kg). Since 2011, two **paleontologists** now believe that an even larger bear once lived in South America: the South American giant short-faced bear. Measuring a fossilized leg bone, they calculated that this bear weighed about 3,500 pounds (1,600 kg). It would have been at least 11 feet (3.5 m) tall when standing on its hind legs. These huge bears became extinct about 10,000 years ago, shortly after the first humans arrived in the Americas.

bear. Cave bears lived in Europe and western Asia. They became extinct around 28,000 years ago, but by that time prehistoric human artists had drawn images of these great creatures on the walls of caves, where they can still be seen today.

Modern Bears

Of the eight bear species alive today, the giant panda of China is descended from a branch of the bear family tree that separated long ago from the rest. The South American spectacled bear is the last survivor of a branch that spread through the Americas and then died out. The other six living bear species are descended from the small *Ursus minimus.*

As bears moved into different parts of the world, they evolved to fit new **habitats** and ways of life. This led to variety among modern bear species. Pandas are large, slow-moving bamboo eaters. Spectacled bears are medium-sized bears that live in moist forests on the slopes of the Andes Mountains in western South America. Their diet is mostly plant foods such as fruit, nuts, flowers, and bark, but they also prey on rabbits, mice, birds, and occasionally larger animals such as cattle.

The sloth bear of India is active at night and feeds mainly on insects, such as termites and honeybees. It is a good climber and goes up trees to seek insect prey. The sun bear is found in tropical forests in Southeast Asia. The smallest living bear species, it eats mostly insects and fruit and has been called the honey bear because of its fondness for bees, beehives, and honey. The Asiatic black bear is a medium-sized bear found in the Himalaya Mountains, China, eastern Russia, Korea, and northern Japan. It spends as much as half of each day in trees. Like nearly all bears, the Asian black bear is an omnivore, feeding on fruit, insects, seeds, nuts, grasses, and prey such as deer and wild cattle.

A brown, or grizzly, bear in Montana.

The American black bear lives in many parts of North America, from Alaska and Canada to Mexico. This bear is most often found in forests and is good at climbing trees and swimming. American black bears eat many kinds of food, including grasses, bulbs, fruit, nuts, and acorns, and prey such as deer, rodents, fish, elk, and moose.

Another omnivore is the brown bear, sometimes called the grizzly in the United States. This species has a wide **range**, meaning that it is found across a large area of the world. Brown bears are native to Europe, Asia, and North America. They were also once found in Mexico and in the mountains of North Africa, but those populations of brown bears are almost certainly extinct.

The brown bears that live on Kodiak Island and a few other islands off the south coast of Alaska are known as Kodiak bears. There are more than a dozen varieties of brown bears in the world, but Kodiak bears are the largest—almost as big as polar bears. In fact, brown bears and polar bears are very closely related.

The shaggy-haired sloth bear of India is most likely descended from brown bears.

The ABC Bears

A piece of the polar bear puzzle lives on three islands off the southeast coast of Alaska. This part of Alaska is home to grizzlies, but the bears that live on Admiralty, Baranof, and Chichagof Islands—known as the ABC bears—are a special group. Their genetic makeup is different enough from all other brown bears that scientists think the ABC bears have been evolving on their own, apart from other brown bears, for a long time.

A small part of the ABC bear genetic makeup is the same as that of the polar bear. Does this mean that polar bears evolved from the ABC bears? Not necessarily. The ABC bears may have evolved from a population of polar bears that lived on the Admiralty, Baranof, and Chichagof Islands during a past ice age, when the climate of southeast Alaska was icy and cold. The ice melted, but the polar bears remained on the islands. Over time, female polar bears mated with male brown bears that swam to the islands, and the ABC bears are their descendants.

Seeking the Origin of Polar Bears

The story of the polar bear starts with the brown bear, its closest relative. For years, scientists have been sure that polar bears evolved from brown bears. The territories of brown bears and polar bears sometimes overlap, and the two species are still so close that they sometimes interbreed, both in zoos and in the wild.

The offspring of these matings are hybrids, part polar bear and part brown bear. Unlike some hybrids (such as mules, which are the offspring of horses and donkeys), hybrid polar-brown bears are fertile, which means that they can produce offspring of their own.

Where, when, and how did the evolutionary shift from brown bears to polar bears take place? Scientists have not found it easy to answer those questions.

One problem is that fossils of polar bears are rare. Scientists have been able to study plenty of fossils of European cave bears because those bears lived (and died) in caves. They left skeletal remains in places where the bones would fossilize and where paleontologists could easily uncover them. Polar bears, however, spend a lot of time on floating ice. Their remains are usually lost at sea.

Fossils of early polar bears are so rare that there was much excitement in the scientific world when a polar bear jawbone and tooth were found in 2004 in Svalbard, an island group that is the most northern part of Norway. These polar bear remains are between 110,000 and 130,000 years old—the oldest polar bear remains ever found.

The Svalbard remains were not completely fossilized, and researchers managed to get strands of DNA from them. The DNA showed that the Svalbard bear, although it looked like a polar bear and lived in a polar

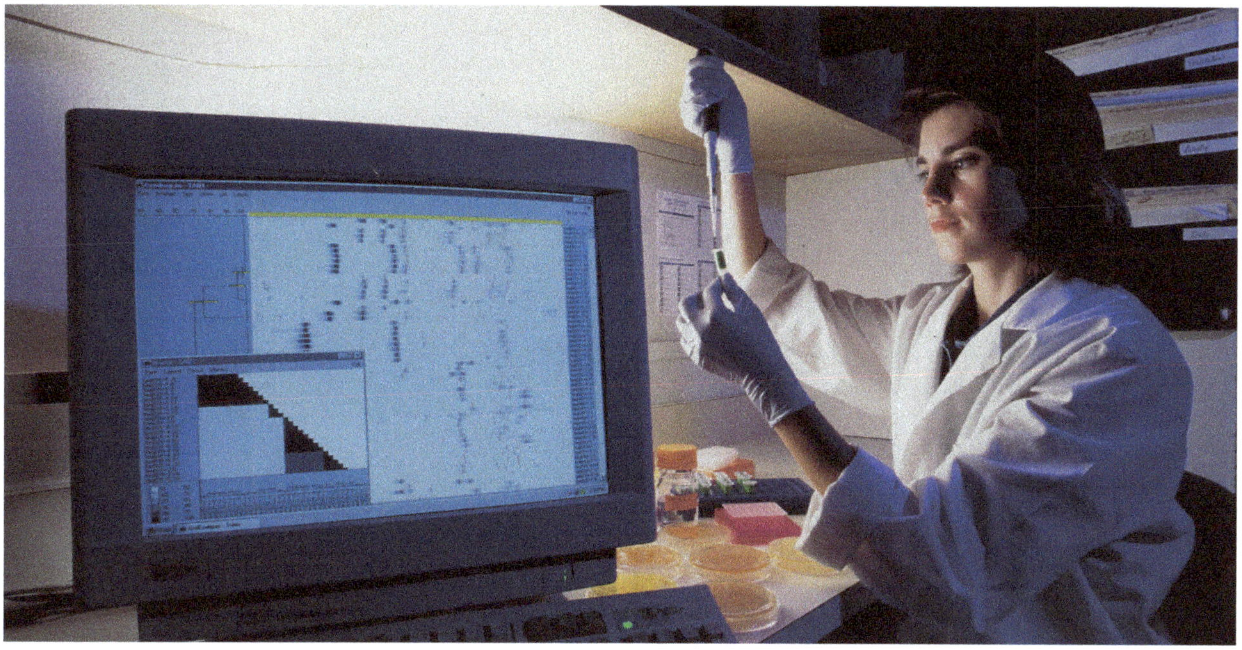

A researcher prepares a DNA sample for testing. Genetic research has brought new discoveries about bears.

bear's habitat, had some of the same genetic material as a brown bear. This led the researchers to think that the jawbone and tooth came from a polar bear that lived not long after polar bears had split away from brown bears.

Based on this evidence, the researchers concluded that the ancestors of polar bears began separating from brown bears around 150,000 years ago, and that it took the new species just 10,000 to 30,000 years to evolve into polar bears. Then, in 2012 and 2013, several teams of scientists revealed the results of new, more complete studies of bear DNA. These studies suggest that polar bears and brown bears have been two separate species for much longer—anywhere from 500,000 to several million years.

While DNA discoveries have pushed polar bear origins further into the past, wildlife biologists are learning more all the time about the magnificent polar bears of the present.

CHAPTER TWO

FUR, FANGS, AND MORE

The polar bear's scientific name is *Ursus maritimus*, which means "bear of the sea." In the languages of various countries, the polar bear has also been called "ice bear," "snow bear," and "white bear." All of these names are true. The polar bear dwells on or near the sea, amid ice and snow. Inside and out, the polar bear is beautifully adapted to life in this harsh, cold habitat.

Dressed for Snow

For birds and animals that live in snowy or icy environments, white coloring serves as **camouflage**. It helps the birds or animals blend into the background. Blending in is useful for hiding from **predators** and from prey. The snowy owl of the far north has white or mostly white feathers. The Arctic fox is brown in the summer, but turns white in the winter. And while the polar bear is another creature of the north that is known for its white coat, in reality, its fur is not white—it is shiny and clear, like glass. It looks white because of the way it scatters light.

Adult polar bears don't have to worry about predators. They're the biggest, most dangerous hunters in their environment (except for humans armed with guns). A polar bear's coat does not often appear pure white. It usually looks cream-colored or pale yellow. Still, it does not stand out against a background of snow the way a brown or black coat would. By making them hard to see against a white background, the polar bears' coloring helps them ambush or sneak up on unsuspecting prey.

Polar bear fur has two layers. The underfur is thick and soft, with hairs up to two inches long. The guard hair layer is longer and rougher. Guard hairs are usually around 6 inches (15.24 cm) long, but some male polar bears have much longer, shaggier guard hairs on the backs of their front legs. This shaggy leg hair may serve the same purpose as the mane of a male lion, which attracts females.

Guard hairs are hollow, like narrow tubes with air inside them. These air spaces trap heat and help insulate the bear, or keep it warm. The trapped air also adds buoyancy, helping to support the bear's weight when it is in water, like thousands of tiny inner tubes.

While the coat of the polar bear has evolved to protect it as it swims in icy-cold water, very young bears are not born with their protective, insulating guard hairs—these hairs grow in as they mature. Mother bears try to keep their small cubs from getting wet, because a wet cub may die of exposure to the cold.

Hair grows thickly on a polar bear's feet, between the toes and around the fleshy, cushion-like footpads. Those hairy feet are another adaptation to a life lived in snow and ice. The hair not only keeps their feet warm but also adds traction, or grip, on slippery surfaces. The footpads are covered with tiny bumps that add more traction. The claws of a polar bear are shorter and sharper than those of a grizzly. The bear uses them for traction, climbing on ice, and for seizing prey.

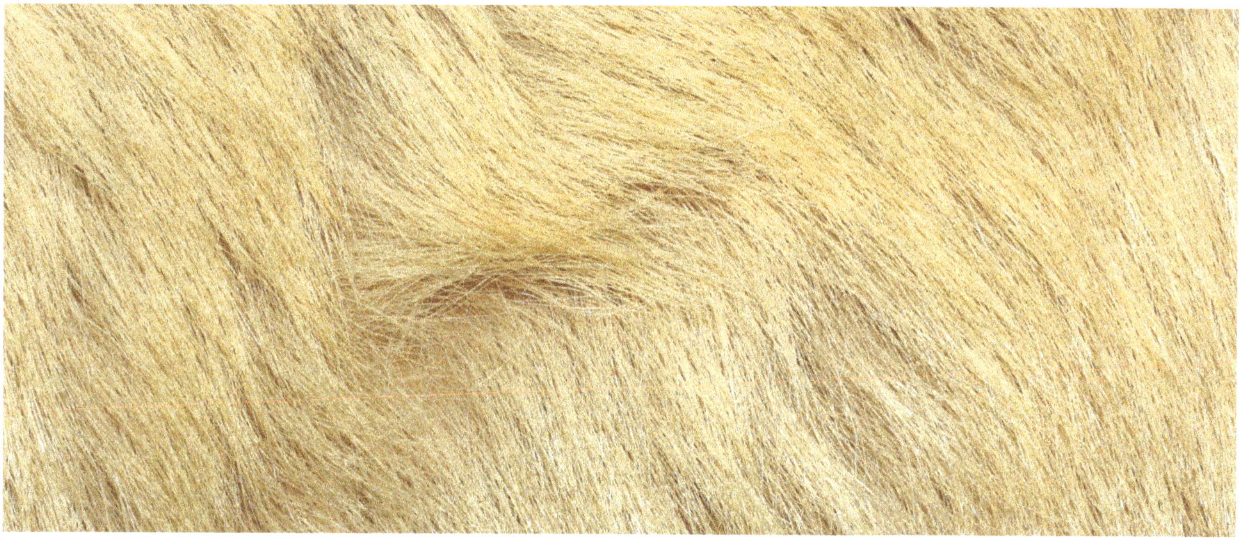

Even though it is not really white, a polar bear's pale fur camouflages it on the arctic ice.

Polar Bear Anatomy

Claws are not a polar bear's only tools for catching prey. Many features of the bear's **anatomy**, or physical structure, have evolved for stalking and catching animals such as ringed seals, the polar bear's most common prey.

A polar bear's head is longer and narrower than a grizzly's head. Scientists think that the shape of the polar bear's head, as well as its long neck, help it to reach through holes in the ice to snatch seals, and to probe into the ice caves where seals give birth to their pups. The polar bear's long canine teeth—the four fangs in the front of its mouth—are for gripping prey. The side teeth, or molars, are for cutting and chewing it.

Polar bear molars are taller and sharper than grizzly molars, which makes them better at shearing chunks of meat. Grizzly molars can tear and chew meat, but they are better than polar bear molars at grinding and chewing vegetation. Grizzly teeth are ideal for an omnivore, but polar bear teeth have changed to better fit the life of a carnivore.

Green Bears?

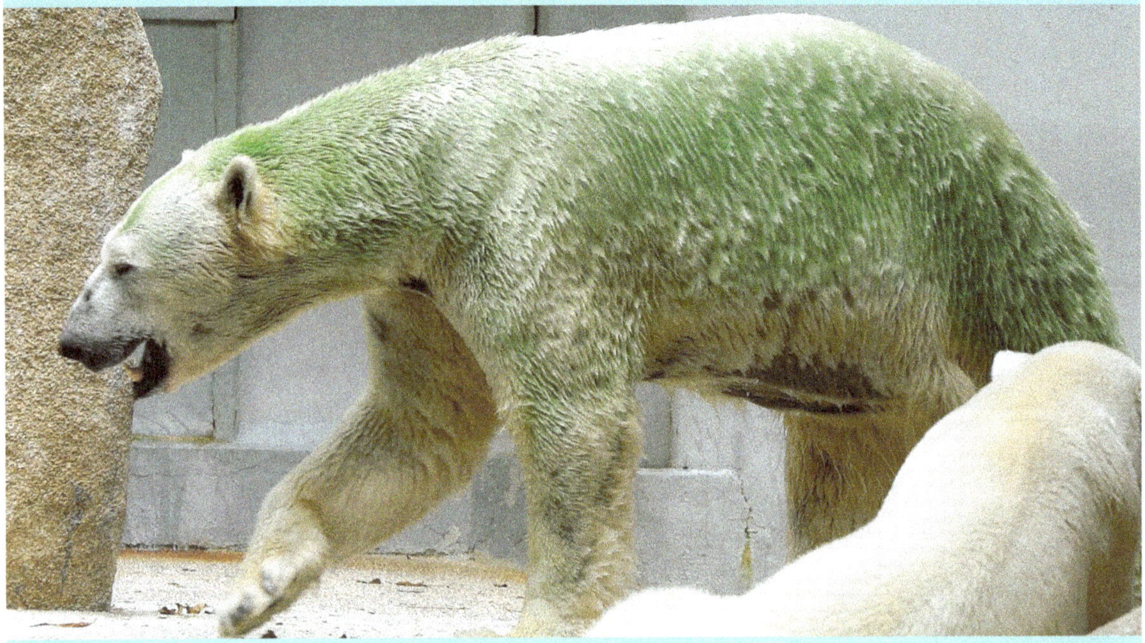

Visitors to some zoos have been surprised by the sight of bright green polar bears. The strange color is caused by algae, a microscopic green plant growing inside the hollow guard hairs of the bears. In zoos, the water provided for polar bears to swim in is usually warmer than the water in the bears' natural habitat. Algae can live in this warmer water, and it can get inside the guard hairs when the bears swim. The warmth and moisture inside the hairs creates the perfect environment for algae to thrive.

Fortunately for the bears, the startling emerald hue does them no harm. After zookeepers get rid of the algae in the bears' swimming ponds, the bears gradually lose their green tint and return to normal.

The large body size of polar bears gives them an advantage in a cold climate by letting them store a lot of fat. The bears' diet is rich in protein and in fat from seal blubber. The fat the bears pack onto their sturdy frames serves two purposes. It is stored energy, and it is insulation, helping to keep the bears warm.

A polar bear stores most of its extra fat in its rear end, near the base of its tail. In times of good hunting, with plenty to eat, a bear can increase its weight by as much as 50 percent through stored fat. A fat bear, however, cannot run as fast as a leaner bear, which can reach speeds of up to 20 miles (32.2 km) an hour for short distances.

Polar bears are much like other bears on the inside, except for their kidneys and their liver. These organs have evolved to meet the special needs of the sea bear.

As in all animals, the job of the kidneys is to filter out wastes and harmful substances from the animal's bloodstream so that they can

A male polar bear surveys his territory on pack ice near Svalbard, Norway.

be sent out of the body in urine. Salt is one of the substances that the kidneys filter. Because polar bears' diet includes a lot of salt from seals, fish, and other saltwater-dwelling prey, their kidneys have to handle a lot of salt. The kidneys are covered with many bumps and ridges that enlarge the organs' working area.

The liver is another organ that filters blood, removing and storing harmful substances. One material stored in the liver is vitamin A, which can be dangerous in large doses. Since seals, the bears' main food source, are high in vitamin A, polar bear livers have to store twenty to a hundred times as much vitamin A as human livers do.

Eating a polar bear's liver can make a person severely sick from an overdose of vitamin A. It can even be fatal, as explorers who feasted on polar bear liver tragically discovered. Polar bears can handle the high amount of vitamin A, however. Their livers have a large number of special fatty cells that absorb the vitamin A and protect the bears from its harmful effects.

Senses and Sounds

Relative to the size of its head, a polar bear's ears are smaller than the ears of other bears. Small ears are another feature of life in a cold climate. A smaller surface area makes it easier for the circulating blood to keep the ears warm. This means that the ears will lose less heat to the surrounding cold air. Even with small ears, polar bears have sharp hearing. They are especially good at picking up the low-pitched barks, yelps, and other sounds made by seals.

Scientists do not yet know whether polar bears have vision that is better, worse, or about the same as human vision. The bears do have better night vision than humans—a definite advantage in the far

Hunters have reported polar bears that cover their noses with their paws while waiting for prey. Are the bears trying to blend into the white background? Scientists do not know.

north, where night's darkness can last for weeks or months. Scent, however, is probably the polar bear's most valuable sense. All species of bears rely on their sense of smell to locate not just food but also other bears, including their mates and offspring.

Polar bears communicate with each other through sounds, such as the puffing or blowing noise that a bear makes as a warning when it feels angry or threatened. They also growl, roar, and make moaning sounds. Cubs are more "talkative" than adults. One researcher heard a lost cub making a sound that he described as a long "maaaaw." The cry could be heard from half a mile away—and drew the mother back to the lost cub.

CHAPTER THREE

THE LIFE OF A POLAR BEAR

Since the 1980s, scientists have learned a great deal about polar bears by using tools such as radio tags to track bears' movements and video cameras to film their activities. Much remains to be learned, but experts in ursine studies now know more than ever before about where polar bears live, what they eat, and how they raise their cubs.

Around the Arctic

Polar bears live in the northernmost part of the world: the Arctic Circle and regions next to it. They are a **circumpolar** (meaning "around the pole") species because they live all around the North Pole. The range of the polar bear reaches into five countries: Norway, Russia, the United States, Canada, and Denmark (which owns the island of Greenland near Canada). These nations have signed the International Agreement on the Conservation of Polar Bears, a plan for the nations to work together to study polar bears and govern the hunting of the bears.

Scientists have identified nineteen populations of polar bears around the Arctic. Each population is made up of bears that live in a particular area, such as Southern Hudson Bay in Canada, the Laptev Sea north of Russia, the Chukchi Sea between Russia and Alaska, or the Arctic Basin around the North Pole.

Bears from one population sometimes mingle with those of a neighboring population, but for the most part, the bears in each area remain within that area. All nineteen population areas share certain features. Each of them includes at least some land, whether it is a handful of Arctic islands or the edge of a continent. More important, each population area contains a lot of sea ice.

The Importance of Sea Ice

Sea ice is frozen seawater, floating on the ocean, free of land. The world of the polar bear is the cap of sea ice at the top of the world, bordered by islands, continents, and open water. The Arctic sea ice grows larger each winter and shrinks each summer. In all of recorded history, it has not disappeared completely.

Sea ice moves with the water beneath it. Currents, tides, and winds can shift and shape huge expanses of sea ice. Lanes of open water called leads can open and then close suddenly. The thickness of the ice varies—it can be piled up into huge ridges or melted down into thin floating sheets, depending on the season and the currents.

The primary habitat of polar bears is sea ice over the fairly shallow water at the edges of the continents, not over the great depths at the center of the Arctic Basin. The edge of the Arctic Ocean is where most polar bears are found.

Some bears spend their entire lives on the ice and never set a paw on land. Others spend part of each year on land. The bears of the Western Hudson Bay population, for example, live on the sea ice of Hudson Bay until it breaks up and melts in the spring. They then migrate onto land and spend their summers there, waiting for the ice

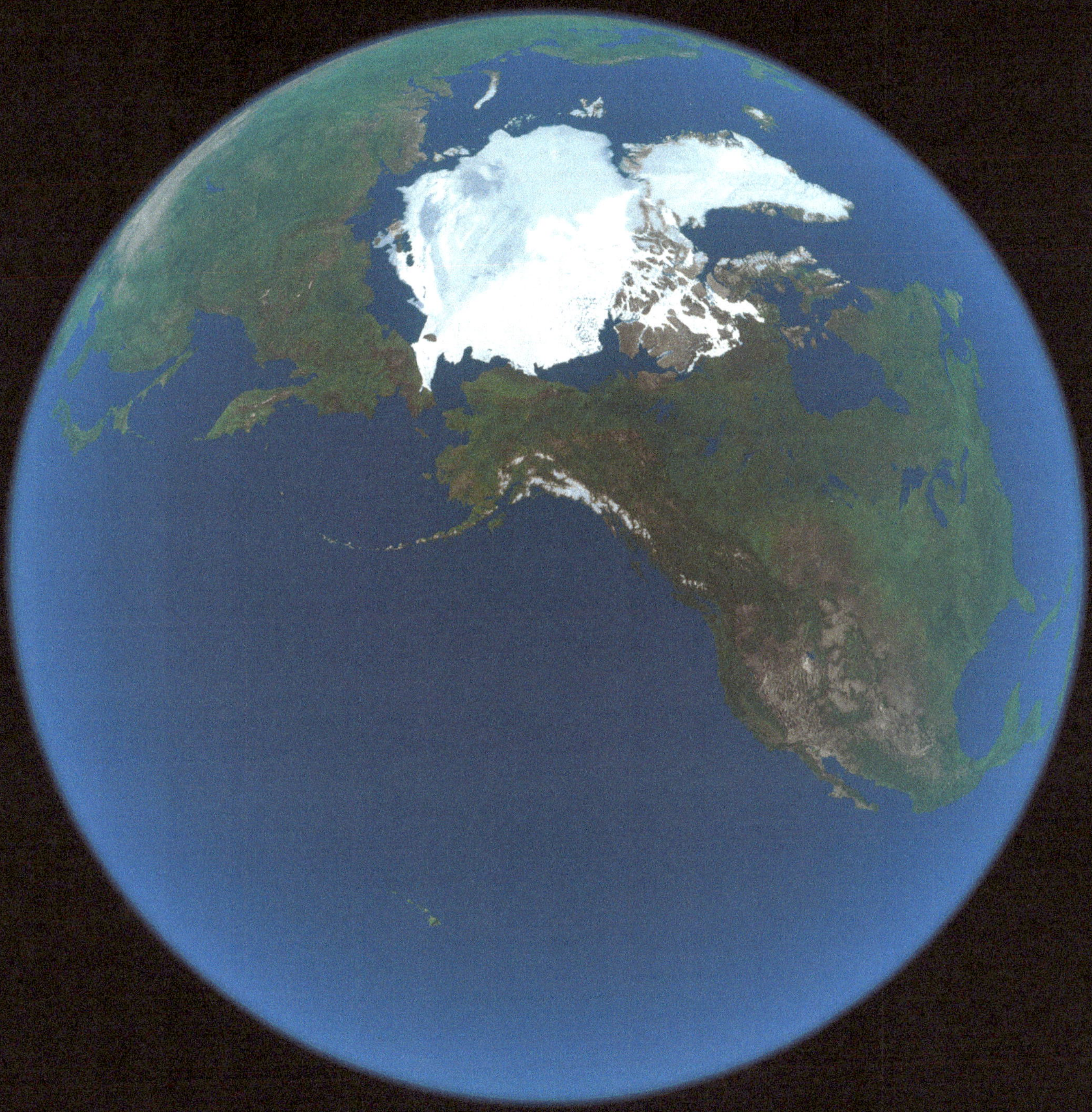

Summer ice over the Arctic region, the home of the polar bear. In winter the ice reaches farther south.

to form again in the fall. So many of these bears can be seen near the town of Churchill, Manitoba, that it calls itself the Polar Bear Capital of the World.

Bears that live farther north have a different way of coping with summer. When the sea ice begins to break up around the edges of the ice pack, they retreat north onto thicker ice, returning to the southern fringes of the sea ice in the fall.

Hunting and Feeding

Polar bears' primary prey are seals that live in icy water, such as ringed and bearded seals. These seals have thick layers of blubber, or fat, which is a major, high-energy portion of a polar bear's diet. A bear will often devour the blubber from a carcass and leave the meat to be scavenged by Arctic foxes and gulls.

This bear will feast on the fatty blubber of the young bearded seal. Blubber is a vital part of the polar bear diet.

Any opening in the sea ice may be a breathing spot for seals—and an ambush spot for bears.

Bears do stalk and hunt prey, but a favorite hunting method is to lie in wait near a crack or hole in the ice, waiting for a seal to stick its head up out of the water to breathe. Because seals must breathe regularly, they keep breathing holes open by poking them with their heads and scratching them with their flippers. Bears know that such holes are good places to snatch a meal. As soon as a seal's head pops up for air, the bear makes a quick grab. Bears spend more than half their time hunting, but only about one of every fifty attempts actually snags them a meal.

Polar bears also prey on other species of seals and, less often, on larger **marine** mammals such as walrus and beluga whales, especially if the whales are stranded on shore. They also kill reindeer, caribou, fish, and ducks and other seabirds. On land, they eat the eggs of snow geese, as well as berries, grass, and moss. Such meals provide little nutrition to an animal that evolved to be a blubber-eating carnivore, however. Although bears turn to land-based foods in times of need, those foods alone will not support a population of polar bears.

Hibernating or Not?

Hibernation allows an animal to save its energy and escape harsh weather. Grizzly bears, for example, hibernate, stuffing themselves with food in the fall and then spending the winter asleep in a [illegible] hibernate. They enter a state of light or shallow hibernation, with a slower heart rate and a slightly lower body temperature than normal. A pregnant female may remain inactive for as long as eight months without eating, drinking, or eliminating waste. This reduces her energy needs by up to 60 percent, so that more energy can go to her unborn or newborn cubs.

In addition, any polar bear with enough stored fat can enter a state that biologists call "walking hibernation" when food is scarce or not available. In this state, the bear moves around normally while chemicals in its body turn waste in its bloodstream into energy. In this way, it does not destroy its own kidneys and muscles due to lack of food.

Family Life

Polar bears are sometimes described as solitary, meaning that they spend most of their time alone rather than in packs. This is true of other bears as well. Polar bears, however, are not complete loners.

Bears may gather at times and places where they know there will be good hunting, such as the birthing grounds of seals. With no shortage of food, there is no need for them to fight. For example, thirty or more bears have been spotted feeding on a single whale carcass. A dozen or more male bears may also hang out together near Churchill during the ice-free summer, resting in shallow pits just a few yards apart and even play-fighting, a type of wrestling that produces no serious injuries.

Fighting turns serious in breeding season, which takes place on the sea ice in spring, when seal hunting is at its height. Fights between males for the right to mate with a female can lead to serious injuries, and most adult males bear the scars of at least one such fight. Males begin breeding at around seven to ten years of age, and females at around five.

Once a male has mated with a female, he plays no further role in family life. The pregnant female eats as much as possible for a few months, and then retreats into a den where she will wait until her cubs are born. Often the den is a cave in a snowdrift on land, close to the coast, but some females carve their dens out of snow on the sea ice. A female bear may use the same den year after year, or find an unused den and make it her own.

The den usually has several tunnels leading into and out of it. It must be big enough for the mother bear to move around, yet small enough to provide insulation for the cubs, who are born in winter.

Polar bears usually give birth to two cubs at a time. The newborns are small (about 2 pounds; 1 kg) and very sensitive to cold. The mother's primary job for several months is to keep her young warm while nourishing them with milk from her mammary glands.

A few months after the cubs are born, the mother bear breaks out of the den, and the cubs see the outside world for the first time. The family spends several weeks close to the den while the cubs learn their way around. Then the mother leads them out to the seal-hunting grounds on the sea ice. By this time, she may have been without food for as long as eight months.

Polar bear cubs usually remain with their mothers for two years or so, learning how to hunt and scavenge food and how to travel across the sea ice. The mother will chase them away when she is ready to mate again and start a new family. If both cubs have survived, they may stay together for several years before they start their adult lives.

Polar bears in the wild can live up twenty-five years with a steady food supply. The most common cause of death for old bears is starvation when they become too weak or injured to hunt.

CHAPTER FOUR

FACING THE FUTURE

Polar bears have become a symbol of wildlife in danger. In the eyes of many people, the biggest threat to the bears is **climate change**, which is causing sea ice to shrink and melt. No one likes to picture polar bears starving at sea in their desperate search for ice from which to hunt, or cubs dying of cold because the ice has become too thin to support them and they plunge into the frigid water. But how real is the threat?

Understanding Climate Change

The world is changing. The Intergovernmental Panel on Climate Change (IPCC), which consists of some of the world's top scientists, has gathered evidence to show beyond a doubt that our planet is getting warmer. This warming trend, called climate change, is also often referred to as global warming. By measuring the temperatures of samples of air and seawater, the IPCC has determined that the Earth's average temperature overall has increased by 1.4 degrees Fahrenheit (0.8° degrees Celsius) over the past 100 years. While the Earth's climate naturally fluctuates over time, scientists are alarmed by the current climate change trend because of how quickly it is happening.

There is some debate about what is causing this global trend. However, there is a huge amount of evidence pointing to a buildup of **greenhouse gases**, such as carbon dioxide (CO_2) and methane. These gases are often created by power plants and cars that run on fossil fuels, such as gas or coal. When these gases are released into the atmosphere they absorb radiation from the sun and prevent it from escaping, causing an overall warming of the Earth's climate. This is called the **greenhouse effect**. Just like the warm, humid climate in a greenhouse, Earth's atmosphere is trapping heat rather than letting it exit.

Climate scientists have found that ice cores from the Arctic and Antarctic help measure the amount of greenhouse gases in the atmosphere in a given year. During winter freezes, ice cores actually trap and preserve samples of the atmosphere, creating a record of the makeup of Earth's atmosphere stretching back many decades. When climate scientists analyzed the data retrieved from several ice cores found in Greenland and Antarctica, they discovered that higher amounts of greenhouse gasses found in the cores were also the years with higher than average recorded temperatures.

While this trend may prove dangerous for all forms of life on Earth, including humans, polar bears who make their homes on frozen ice seem to be especially at risk.

A Changing Habitat

One result of global warming is a change in the Arctic sea ice. The U.S. National Oceanic and Atmospheric Administration (NOAA) monitors the size of the Arctic sea ice every year, recording its growth and melting through satellite images. In 2012, NOAA reported that the total area of the sea ice was smaller in September, the end of the melting season, than in any year since 1979, when satellite monitor-

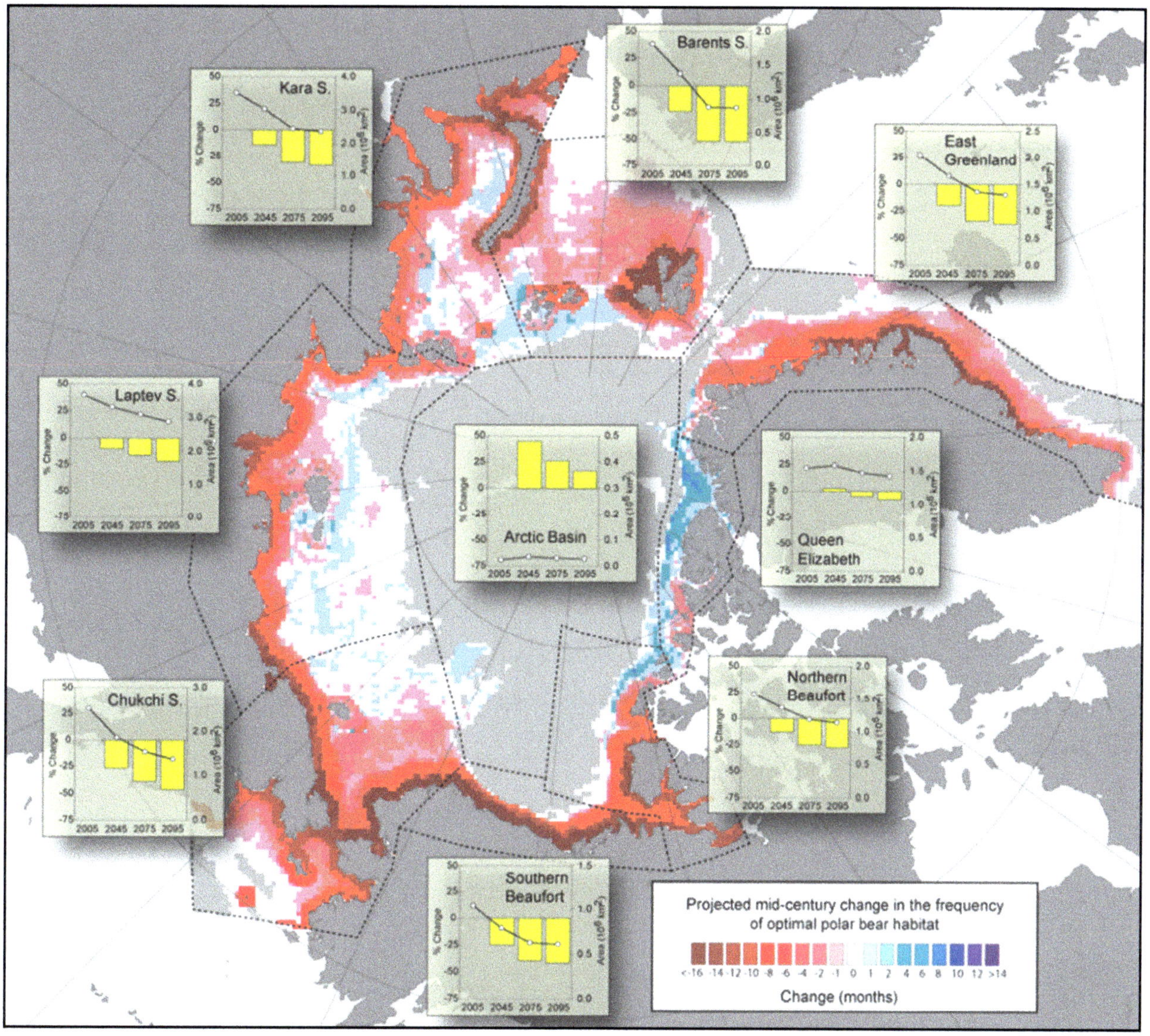

Based on trends in melting and freezing sea ice, the U.S. Geological Survey projects how polar bears' habitat around the Arctic Basin will change by the 2040s. Red areas are expected to lose good bear habitat, blue areas to gain it. The small charts in each region show the overall amount of habitat (lines) and the degree of change from 2001 to 2050 (yellow bars).

ing began. NOAA also reported that the thick ice in the center of the Arctic Basin, which does not disappear from year to year, was growing thinner.

Scientists at the National Air and Space Administration (NASA) agree. They reported in 2013 that the Arctic is losing about 30,000 square miles (78,000 sq. km) of sea ice a year. That's an area the size of Maine. Many experts in climate science fear that—even with the occasional extra-cold year and extra-large ice pack—the trend toward shrinking sea ice will continue. NASA researchers used to think that the Arctic could lose all of its sea ice in summer by the end of the twenty-first century. Now they fear that the Arctic could see ice-free summers by the middle of the century.

What would this mean for the polar bear? Less sea ice means less habitat, and less area in which to hunt. It means that bears—including cubs—may face longer swims between patches of ice. It also means that bears may move out of their usual areas in search of food. People in some communities in the far north have already reported seeing more bears than usual. However, Canadian biologist Andrew E. Derocher, one of the world's leading experts on polar bears, points out that the idea that polar bears could "adapt" to life on land if the sea ice disappears is "nonsense." Even at its fastest, evolution cannot redesign the polar bear in a century—or less.

Polar Bears and People

Climate change and shrinking sea ice are not the only dangers to polar bears. Human activities have created other threats.

People have hunted polar bears for as long as people have lived in the Arctic. In modern times, however, the hunt changed. High-powered rifles and helicopters let hunters slaughter far more bears than ever before. For years bears were killed by remote control, as hunters set up rifles inside boxes baited with meat. When a hungry bear tugged at the bait, it was blasted by the rifle. These "self-killing guns," as they were called, are now banned, as is hunting bears from helicopters or planes.

Are Polar Bears Endangered?

An endangered species is one that is at real risk of disappearing from the wild. In the United States, the federal government determines whether a species is in trouble and needs to be covered by the Endangered Species Act (ESA). The United States declared in 2008 that polar bears are "threatened" across their entire range because of the loss of their sea ice habitat. "Threatened" means that a species is not yet endangered, but is likely to become so.

The International Union for the Conservation of Nature (IUCN) is a worldwide collection of scientists and researchers that studies the health of thousands of species. The IUCN lists polar bears as "vulnerable," which means the same thing as "threatened"—one level below "endangered." According to the IUCN, of the nineteen polar bear populations in the world, eight are growing smaller, three are stable, and one is increasing. There is not enough information about the other seven populations to know whether they are shrinking or growing. The IUCN's best estimate of the total number of polar bears in the world is 20,000 to 25,000.

Although polar bear numbers are not falling in some parts of their range, the overall, long-term picture is not so good. Experts agree that these mighty bears of the far north are at risk, and the most serious threat they face is a warming world.

Traditional hunting communities still eat polar bear meat and wear skins.

Every nation except Norway, however, does allow some hunting of polar bears, either for sport or by people for whom such hunting is a tradition. In traditional communities in Greenland, for example, people eat polar bear meat and wear clothing made of polar bear hides. Conservationists hope to pass an international ban on commercial trade of the hides, so that polar bear products will be used only in traditional communities and not sold on the open market. This could reduce the killing of bears.

Pollution is a more serious problem than hunting. “There is no such thing,” says polar bear expert Derocher, “as an unpolluted polar bear.” Toxic chemicals from factories, coal-fired electrical plants, and farms travel for thousands of miles into the Arctic, carried on winds and ocean currents. Because polar bears are at the top of the Arctic food web, these harmful substances build up in the bears’ bodies. Pollutants are stored in seal fat and then in the bodies of the bears that eat the seals. Even newborn cubs have been found to have high levels of dangerous pollutants, such as mercury and lead, fed to them in their mothers' milk. These pollutants have been shown to interfere with the bears' kidneys and nervous systems.

Development in the north is another possible threat. With rising temperatures and melting ice, some people call for increased oil drilling and mining in the Arctic. Ship traffic is also likely to increase, bringing further pollution and disruption.

For thousands of years, polar bears have flourished in a silent, white, cold world far from most human activity. But without a different kind of human activity—action to stop the warming of the planet and preserve the Arctic—the biggest bear on Earth may lose its habitat and be known to future generations only in zoos.

Hot exhaust spills into the air from an oil-processing plant in northern Alaska. Conservationists warn that increased drilling for oil and gas in the Arctic may damage the habitats of many species.

GLOSSARY

anatomy - the shape and structure of a living thing and its parts

camouflage - coloring or patterning that helps an animal blend into its natural background

canid - member of the dog family

carnivore - meat-eater

circumpolar - around the pole; the polar bear's range is circumpolar because it surrounds the North Pole

climate change - the overall warming trend of the Earth's atmosphere

DNA - deoxyribonucleic acid, a genetic material within the cells of living things that carries traits and features from one generation to the next

evolve - to change slightly from one generation to another; over time, this change, called evolution, creates new species of animals and plants

fossil - all or part of an ancient plant or animal, preserved in stone

genetic - having to do with genes and the DNA of which genes are made; each species has it own genetic makeup, or genome

genus - group of closely related species

greenhouse effect - the trapping of the sun's warmth in the Earth's atmosphere

greenhouse gases - gases such as carbon dioxide (CO_2) and methane that contribute to climate change

habitat - type of setting or environment in which an animal lives; for example, the polar bear's habitat is Arctic sea ice or coastal areas with significant snow and ice

hemicyonid - member of an extinct group of animals also called "half-dogs" or "bear-dogs," with features of both dogs and bears

mammal - animal that gives birth to live young and feeds the young from milk glands in the mother's body

marine - having to do with the ocean

omnivore - animal that eats both meat and plant foods

paleontologist - scientist who studies ancient or extinct life forms, usually by examining fossil remains

predator - animal that lives by killing and eating other animals; a hunter

range - part of the world in which a plant or an animal species lives; a range can be as large as the entire planet or as small as a single tree

species - kind of animal or plant; a species includes all the individual animals or plants that can interbreed with each other

ursid - member of the bear family

ursine - like a bear, or related to bears

FIND OUT MORE

Books

Hirsch, Rebecca E. *Top 50 Reasons to Care About Polar Bears.* Berkeley Heights, NJ: Enslow, 2010.

Lourie, Peter. *The Polar Bear Scientists.* Boston, MA: Houghton Mifflin Books for Children, 2012.

Middleton, Don. *Polar Bears.* New York, NY: AV2 Books, 2013.

Olson, Gillia M. *Polar Bears' Search for Ice.* Mankato, MN: Capstone, 2011.

Websites

Polar Bears International

www.polarbearsinternational.org/about-polar-bears/essentials

A top conservation group devoted to studying and saving polar bears offers information to students and teachers.

Polar Bear

animals.nationalgeographic.com/animals/mammals/polar-bear

National Geographic's web page about polar bears has basic information and an audio clip of a polar bear's roar.

More Websites

Fact Sheet: Polar Bear

www.defenders.org/polar-bear/basic-facts

The Defenders of Wildlife web page pulls together facts about polar bears and links to a video and articles about the bears and their changing habitat.

Polar Bears

www.panda.org/what_we_do/where_we_work/arctic/wildlife/polar_bear

The World Wildlife Fund's polar bear page has an interview with an expert on polar bears and a link to a live tracker that allows online visitors to follow the movements of polar bears.

The Environmental Protection Agency Climate Change Home Page

epa.gov/climatechange

Find out more about climate change, its causes and effects, and what you can do to help.

INDEX

Page numbers in **boldface** are illustrations.

ABOUT THE AUTHOR

Rebecca Stefoff has published more than a hundred books for young readers. Although she has written about many topics in history and science, writing about biology and nature is one of her specialties. Among her books on animal life is *Bears* (Marshall Cavendish Benchmark, 2002), a detailed look at the evolution, anatomy, and life cycles of all species of bears that live in the world today. Stefoff has been lucky enough to see black bears in the wild while hiking and camping—always from a safe distance, fortunately. She lives in the Pacific Northwest, where she enjoys outdoor activities such as hiking, bicycling, and birding. One of her dreams is to travel in the Arctic, where, if she is lucky, she might glimpse a polar bear, the mightiest bear of all—again, she hopes, from a safe distance.